PRACTICAL *Joy*

# PRACTICAL
## Joy

SIMPLE TOOLS TO CULTIVATE
MORE JOY EVERY DAY

M. Shannon Hernandez

Practical Joy: Simple Tools to Cultivate More Joy Everyday
Published by PRACTICAL JOY MEDIA
Edgewater, New Jersey, U.S.A.

HERNANDEZ, M. SHANNON, Author
PRACTICAL JOY
M. SHANNON HERNANDEZ

Library of Congress Control Number: 2022916341

ISBN: 979-8-218-06720-5

BODY, MIND & SPIRIT / Inspiration & Personal Growth
SELF-HELP / Personal Growth / Happiness
BUSINESS & ECONOMICS / Women in Business

Illustrations: M. Shannon Hernandez (joyfulbusinessrevolution.com)
Editing: Amy Scott (nomadeditorial.com)
Book Design: Michelle M. White (mmwbooks.com)
Publishing Manager: Susie Schaefer (finishthebookpublishing.com)
Author Photo: Dana Mangus (danamangus.com)

QUANTITY PURCHASES:
Schools, companies, professional groups, clubs, and other organizations
may qualify for special terms when ordering quantities of this title.
For information, email info@practicaljoybook.com.

This book is printed in the United States of America.

Dedication
This book is dedicated to everyone who has ever been made
to feel like they were too much–or never enough.
~ MSH

*"We create most of our suffering, so it should be logical that we also have the ability to create more joy."*

~ Dalai Lama

Meet Your JOY Catalyst
I am all about that JOY!
...It wasn't always this way...
I had to discover that JOY is an inside job.
JOY can't be "found"...
Because JOY lives inside you!
Thank you for joining me on this JOY journey!
Hi! I'm Shannon!

# Contents

# Take It to the People

This book was conceived in the emergency room in Brooklyn, New York, while I waited for medical care.

Six days prior, I'd gone in for a fairly standard procedure— a hysterectomy. But once they got in there, they found thirty-two fibroids, a right ovary filled with cysts, and a uterus the size of a four-month pregnancy, as well as sticky endometrial lining that had glued my bladder to my uterus. This made the surgery more complicated than usual, but I was assured everything had gone smoothly.

I later learned that mine was the last non-life-threatening surgery the hospital would take for months. COVID-19 had hit New York City and everything was being canceled. I literally went in for surgery in one world, and six hours later I emerged into a drastically different one.

The operating room was a flurry of nervous energy and activity. No one knew what was going on, but you could feel the fear and unease amongst the staff. All of a sudden, everyone was wearing masks and gloves, and I was being asked to wear them too.

My doctor's main goal was to get me out of that surgical ward and back home for recovery, away from the virus that seemed to be taking over the world. I agreed completely, as did my spouse, Maria. Later that same afternoon, once I could urinate on my own and walk, I was released from the hospital and given the doctor's personal email and phone number for daily check-ins. We were grateful to be going home.

Maria became my primary caretaker, and we probably would have fared very well if my recovery had gone as expected. But each day, I felt worse than the day before. Fluid started collecting in places I didn't know were possible (I'll spare you the details), and I couldn't stand up without extreme nausea. I couldn't eat without everything hurting, so I was living those first few days on applesauce and Gatorade. Showering became nearly impossible because lifting my leg over the edge of the tub was excruciating.

My doctor and I were in communication every day, and he was monitoring the situation. On the third day after surgery, when these symptoms just kept worsening, Maria put me in the car with a pillow pressed to my abdomen for comfort and support and drove me back to my doctor in Brooklyn—about an hour's drive from our home in New Jersey. I was green-yellow, I couldn't walk, gallons of fluid were bulging from different parts of my body, and my skin hurt. I cried most of the way there, wondering if I was going to make it through the drive.

When I waddled into the doctor's office with the pillow still pressed to my stomach, my doctor met me at the door and immediately yelled to the office staff, "Get me a wheelchair, and get her to the ER, stat." I haven't spent a lot of time in doctor's offices, but I definitely knew this was not normal.

I was wheeled across the street to the ER and saw the sidewalk, lobby, and hallways filled with people in masks and gloves, coughing and sneezing, fear in their eyes. I remember closing my eyes as they wheeled me to reception, because I was scared to look at what was happening around me. The virus was three days old in this city, and you could feel that the hospital was understaffed, the staff overworked. While everyone was doing the best they could, no one was prepared for this level of chaos.

It took about two hours for me to be admitted, where I was then placed on a bed in a crowded corridor. A makeshift curtain was pulled around me for semi-privacy, and a team of doctors and interns started working their magic. Oh, the relief of a catheter! (I never thought I'd say that!) Within ten minutes, they had collected over three gallons of retained fluid from my body. The pockets of flesh that had been protruding from my body finally felt relief, and my skin was slowly returning back to where it should have been.

The diagnosis was in: my kidneys had been in extreme failure for the past three days, and I was lucky to be alive. Because of the way my internal organs had adjusted to the fibroids and the sticky endometrial lining over the years, they didn't know how to function now that there was so much space in my abdominal cavity. And once my bladder had been peeled away from my uterus, it didn't remember how to function properly either.

I lay in that corridor for twelve hours, waiting for a room to open up. I watched staff place hazard signs on "rooms" near me that said, "Do not enter. Positive patient." No one had any idea what was going on, and yet the staff was doing the best they could to keep up with the news, the workload, and the fearful patients.

There was one moment, and thankfully it only lasted for a moment, when I thought: *Death would be better than this.* I was staring at the off-white drop ceiling, listening to all the noise and confusion around me, waiting for the medical care I so desperately needed. Tears welled up in my eyes with that singular statement: *Death would be better than this.*

And in the next moment, I heard a voice say to me: *Do more of what matters—and take it to the people.*

Looking back, I know that the wise and loving voice of The Creator saved my sanity and gave me a renewed reason for living.

But at the time I had no idea what this cryptic message meant. I even remember thinking, *What in the actual hell does that mean, and why now? I'm here, literally on a deathbed awaiting care in the middle of a pandemic, and this is the message that has been delivered? What do I even do with this?*

I didn't know what it meant, but it stuck with me. For two years I let that message play on repeat, waiting for the meaning to reveal itself, knowing that I had been given a mission to "take to the people."

That mission became JOY.

I'd been focused on cultivating personal joy for years, and I had started incorporating joy into my work. It finally hit me that THIS is what matters, and what I'm meant to share with others.

So, I started to explore further:

What would it mean to teach joy, live in joy, be joy, and *take joy to the people*?

Why is more joy needed in our lives and across the world?

What effect will joy have on the consciousness of this planet, when we each choose to focus on our joy first, and as a result, naturally spread more joy to those around us?

How does joy differ from happiness?

These questions, among many others, became my life's mission, and it is with great honor that I began to "take it to the people." This book is just one of the ways I'm doing that.

May you dive into *Practical Joy* with an open heart and mind, and give yourself permission to add more joy to your life than you ever thought possible!

# Your Joyful Wake-Up Call

I could simply tell you that life is short, but seeing it laid out visually is even more powerful.

Look at the graphic below. Each of the dots represents a year, and there are eighty of them—the average life expectancy for a human. Let's discover how many years you have left to choose and live in JOY.

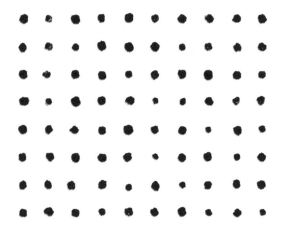

1. Cross out the number of dots/years you have lived already. (To make it easier for you, the dots are arranged in eight rows of ten.)
2. Count the number of dots/years that remain. Divide that number by three. This new number represents the number of years left that you will spend sleeping. Cross off that number of dots/years.
3. Count the remaining dots. This number represents how many years you have LEFT, AWAKE, to live exactly how you want to be living.

I hope this visual makes it clear that you have zero time to waste on things, people, relationships, and experiences that aren't bringing you joy! Your joy matters, and now is the time to make it a priority. Prioritizing your joy is most likely going to require a paradigm shift. A shift that once embraced means there is no going back to un-joy. A shift that will cause you to look at the world differently, look at your relationships differently, and look at your choices differently.

Before I began embodying these *Practical Joy* principles, I found myself continuously searching. Searching for the next experience that would cause my serotonin levels to increase, so that I could feel what I once thought was joy. That beautiful trip to Italy with my mom, the lovely rooftop cocktail in Brooklyn, planning our next date day.

Don't get me wrong—these types of experiences may produce a positive feeling (known as happiness), but it is not joy. Those serotonin spikes are short-lived. This is why I believe so many people actually do not know what true joy is or how to cultivate a life rooted in joy.

This book was designed to give you the tools to experience practical, meaningful, and abundant joy, despite circumstances that may leave you feeling overwhelmed, frustrated, or disconnected.

I am often asked, *How is joy different from happiness?*

If you confuse joy and happiness—well, you'll most likely never experience lasting joy.

Joy is more consistent and is cultivated internally. It comes when you make peace with who you are, why you are, and how you are. Happiness, on the other hand, tends to be externally triggered. It is based on other people, things, places, thoughts, and events.

The simplest way to remember this? Joy is an inside job. Always.

## How I Got Here

For fifteen years, I was a classroom teacher in both Charlotte, North Carolina, and Spanish Harlem, New York City. Middle school students from all walks of life came into my classroom, many checked out and overwhelmed by their everyday circumstances. They thought they were coming to reading and writing class, but they actually stepped through that classroom door into a space of joy. Early in my teaching career, I realized that if I could help the students experience just a little more joy in their day (by guiding them to discover what truly mattered and why), they felt more seen and heard. This resulted in less discipline problems, less parent-teacher meetings, and less disruptions to the curriculum that needed to be taught. It was a win for everyone!

After leaving public education, my joy work continued as a professor at Brooklyn College, and later became the foundation for the work I do with clients in my company, The Joyful Business Revolution™. At the time of writing, we continue to lead the industry with joyful business growth strategy solutions for coaches, consultants, and speakers.

After years of helping business owners develop a revenue growth strategy grounded firmly in joy, I have noticed, once again, how powerful the tools of *Practical Joy* are when applied to businesses and careers, as well as personal lives. The paradigm shift that thousands have gained around joy continues to be profound and personal, and I know this will be the case for you too!

## How to EnJOY This Book

This book was an absolute joy to create. As you flip through the pages, you'll see text, space for writing and capturing your thoughts, and coloring pages, plus some additional "surprises" that I hope will make you smile.

*Practical Joy* will make the most sense if you read the text sequentially, as many of the activities (called Joy Journeys) build upon previous ones.

However, if you need a little joy break in your day, feel free to turn to a random coloring page and connect with the joy of adding color to paper.

Every Joy Journey in this book is tried, true, and tested and offers you practical, relevant, and meaningful ways to access your joy.

The most important aspect to remember is that your joy is a personal journey *and* a daily practice. As you read and interact with the pages of this book, you will understand these concepts on a deeper level.

Welcome to *Practical Joy*. May this book (and way of living) help you experience way more joy in your life and enhance the lives of those around you.

Notes

Notes

# Permission to Think (err... FEEL) Differently

I'm on a mission to spread joy. More joy for you and more joy for me, and using joy as a tool to raise the consciousness of this planet.

I've been doing "joy work" with people for years. And no matter the person, their particular circumstances, or their previous relationship with joy, I continue to hear this feedback over and over again:

> *"You gave me permission to think differently and to choose joy first. Thank you for giving me permission to let go of the things that no longer bring me joy."*

I always find this feedback quite fascinating. I'm grateful for their truth and honored by their words—and I am always a bit taken aback by the "You gave me permission..." sentiment.

Honestly, I don't see myself as a granter of permission, but rather a catalyst to embrace a new way of thinking. A new way of feeling. A new way of choosing. A new way of BEING.

I had a fascinating conversation with a forty-six-year-old woman named Jill who shared that one choice she made twenty years ago changed the trajectory of her entire life. She got married, and also made the choice to not have children. It wasn't easy. Her parents wanted grandchildren. Her parents also *expected* her to have children—hell, let's be honest, *societal norms* (to this day) expect women to get married and have children. (Oy... the heaviness of writing this.)

Jill just didn't want that for herself. The moment she realized that she didn't need to have children to be complete was the exact moment she gave herself permission to live in her full expression of joy. She divorced her husband, chose a different path, and has never regretted that single decision to "start again."

"Start again" and "choose again" are philosophies I live by and encourage others to adopt as well. Because let's be honest here: very few decisions in life are permanent, though they may *feel* permanent when the choice is looming over us, or when we are in the messy middle of emotions, deep thought, and trying to make a decision.

Whenever I am stuck in a quandary, I use these three questions to guide my decision-making:

1. What would feel joyful right now?
2. If I couldn't choose wrong, what would I choose now?
3. What's my next best step from here?

I encourage you to highlight these questions and use them regularly! They really help us make decisions rooted in joy—very quickly.

# Joy Journey
*One*

## Making Decisions Through the Lens of Joy

I'd like you to give this decision-making framework a test run.

What's something you've delayed making a decision about? This works for anything! Maybe it's something as small as what to have for dinner tonight, or something as big as a relationship or career decision.

*Write your quandary/situation here:*

_____

_____

_____

_____

_____

_____

Now, get present to your breath and quiet your mind. And then ask the three questions from your heart-space (not from your head-space). Let your feelings guide your answers. Tap into how you want to feel as you answer each question. Then, jot down your first answers—and don't think yourself out of them!

*1. What would feel joyful right now?*

_____

_____

_____

_____

_____

*2. If I couldn't choose wrong, what would I choose now?*

_____

_____

_____

_____

_____

*3. What's my next best step from here?*

_____

_____

_____

_____

*Whoosh.* Did you feel that?!? I hope so. Congrats!

This is what GIVING YOURSELF permission to tap into your joy looks and feels like. Joyful decision-making stems from powerful questions that you answer from your heart-space.

*So... what did you decide? Write your decision below.*

_____

_____

_____

_____

_____

_____

_____

*Welcome to the joyful side of life!*
*Congrats on giving yourself permission to feel differently,*
*to choose joy first, and to start again when needed.*

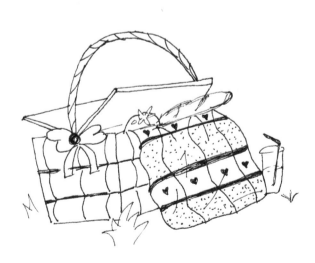

Notes

Notes

Notes

# Joy Is a Choice

## Chapter Two

Joy isn't something that can be chased. Hunted down. Found. Or forced. You can't "pursue" it or blindly discover it. It doesn't just magically appear either.

Joy is a choice.

Joy is cultivated from deep within your soul. It is embodied. You get to choose joy again, and again, and again. You get to experience as much of it as you want. At any time, despite your circumstances.

Bountiful joy grows from a seed you plant in your heart and nurture daily. Not by sitting in meditation, or going on your next dream vacation, or crossing that financial goal off your to-do list. True joy will be yours when you find the courage to pull the weeds of achievement, never-ending to-do lists, and mediocre living.

Ready to plant the seeds and pull the weeds?

It all starts with cultivating a deep connection to your highest lifestyle values and living life accordingly. I'm not talking about values like honesty, integrity, or keeping your word. These are moral values, and while they are important, your lifestyle values are a much different kind of value system to live by.

Once you discover your hierarchy of lifestyle values and use them to make *every* decision, your life will be transformed. You'll rid yourself of the shame, blame, and guilt that cripples so many of us from living the life we truly want to be living. You'll use the word "no" a lot. You'll only be doing the things that light your soul on fire with love and deep connection and that are rooted in meaningful contribution and purpose.

You'll experience more rest, more peace, and a deeper connection to your spirit than ever before.

Other things will happen too as a result of living in your lifestyle values. Your friendships might change. You will make money, effortlessly. You will have way more time for your passion projects and hobbies. You will feel a deep sense of peace in your body, mind, and soul.

When you choose to operate from your hierarchy of lifestyle values, everything shifts. We call this alignment. Decision-making becomes faster and easier. Unlikely relationships form (first with yourself and then with others). You get present to what matters now. You stop chasing short-lived happiness, and you start choosing joy.

I've guided thousands of people to discover *their* unique joy by helping them identify their hierarchy of lifestyle values. Karianne's story is a beautiful one I'd like to share. After two years of navigating the internal struggle of wanting to spend more time with her son, Coen, but knowing that the demands of growing a business required her focus and time, she discovered that her number one lifestyle value was family. Once this became evident, and Karianne made a choice to live by her lifestyle values, everything shifted— without the guilt or shame that so many of us feel when we long to prioritize family over our careers and work. Karianne instituted Coen Wednesdays, which became a joyful way for her and her son to create and share memorable experiences together, each and every Wednesday. And wouldn't you know it—because Karianne is aligned with her joy, her business revenue has significantly increased as well (without needing to work more hours)!

Ready for a personalized experience to discover YOUR joy? Let's go!

## Joy Journey
### *Two*

## Identifying Your Hierarchy of Lifestyle Values

One of the fastest and simplest ways to determine what brings you joy is to look at where you currently spend your time and money. Then, you will examine the shift you may want to make in how you spend your time and money in the near future (like tomorrow—we don't waste time when it comes to getting in alignment!).

### Part 1 - Time and Money

Add entries to each of the following lists. Don't judge anything that surfaces. Don't hold back. Don't censor yourself. Here are a few examples to get you started: I always find time to cook healthy meals, and I always find the money to travel.

*What do you always find the time for?*

1. _____
2. _____
3. _____
4. _____
5. _____
6. _____

*What do you always find the money for?*

1. _____
2. _____
3. _____
4. _____
5. _____
6. _____

## Part 2 - The Shift You Desire

Now, do this exercise again, but project yourself one year into the future. Note: Many of these may be the same as above—that's common. Just go with whatever comes up. Close your eyes, take a few deep breaths, and fill in the lists now.

*What do you always find the time for?*

1. _____
2. _____

3. _____

4. _____

5. _____

6. _____

## *What do you always find the money for?*

1. _____

2. _____

3. _____

4. _____

5. _____

6. _____

## Part 3 - Noticing Themes

Now, the goal is to determine what you already value and what you want more of in the future.

Go through both lists and group items together that relate to each other. What patterns do you see emerging that could help you identify your lifestyle values? Travel? Giving back/volunteering? Relationships? Personal development? Creativity? Health and wellness? Spirituality? Money? Find a word or two to describe each grouping. We call these themes. Once you have identified your themes, list them below.

1. _____

2. _____

3. _____

4. _____

5. _____

6. _____

Now it's time to prioritize your themes to create your hierarchy of values: what is most important to you, followed by the second most important, and so on.

My hierarchy of values looks like this:

1. Health and wellness
2. Travel and experiences
3. Relationships
4. Creativity
5. Nature time

**Note:** You may have only a few themes. That's fine. If you have more than five themes, go back and see which things can be consolidated.

For example:

- "Health and wellness" for me includes spiritual health, mental health, financial health, exercise, massages, eating well, facials, soulful living, etc.
- "Travel and experiences" includes eating out (big foodie here), museums, cultural excursions, road trips

Really think about what is most important to you *right now*. The interesting thing about lifestyle values is they change and evolve as you do. I do this exercise at least twice a year and reorder them as necessary based on what has shifted in my own personal journey.

> *Congrats! You now have your personal hierarchy*
> *of lifestyle values. This is the key to creating*
> *and choosing that deep inner joy in your life.*
> *Now, let's dive in to how to put these into action!*

# Passion Projects

## Chapter Three

Working with people and their joy, I find that many of us have stopped doing things just for fun. Can you relate? I'm sure you know what it feels like to be working and "doing life," and in the process forgetting to live and be passionate about things like gardening, watercolor, reading fiction, and painting rocks.

Yes, you read that correctly! One of my passion projects is painting rocks.

It all started when I lived in Brooklyn and would run in Prospect Park. I realized there was something cool and quirky going on with the local culture there. People would hang lost items on the tree branches, fence posts, or jagged rocks. That pacifier the kid threw out of the stroller? Rock art! That left glove lost by a cyclist? Tree ornamentation. It was such a beautiful and odd part of the local vibe to witness.

Because of this oddity, people had been "trained" to notice and delight in the lost treasures of Brooklyn. There was even a tree in my neighborhood that had hundreds of lost and found doll heads, stuffed animals, and action heroes, commemorating the local childrens' toys. (Not gonna lie, the doll heads dangling from those branches were creepy to look at.)

While running one day, I had a thought: *What if I could spread love and people could find it while they were out and about enjoying the park?* That was how my #LuvRocks project began. I'd collect three smooth rocks each time I ran, paint them in a bright color, and put an inspiring word on the front. And on the back of each rock I'd write: "#LUVROCKS. Pass it on."

Oh, how delightful! I had so much fun painting rocks, planting love on my runs, and then jogging by the following day and noticing they were gone, into the hands of someone who was most likely smiling and spreading joy!

Passion projects. They matter! They fuel our creative spirit, add richness to the fabric of our lives, and keep us from losing our minds.

I often feel a tug-of-war happening when it's time to help people rediscover or find new hobbies and passion projects. They frequently say things like:

- OMG. I don't have time for this.
- I have no idea what I'd do with my free time—I haven't had any for a long time.
- My work is my passion project.

Nope. Hard stop. This is exactly how burnout happens. (I've been here before too!)

We've got to get back to a place where we do things just because, just for fun, just for trying something new and exciting. Please, let's not consider our work/career to be a passion project, no matter how much we love it.

Passion projects help us connect with our joy, and they also have the power to heal us, on many levels.

My client, Stacy, went through a tough time when her father passed away right at the beginning of the pandemic. While grieving her father, lockdown happened, there was no funeral to provide closure, and everything felt really heavy in the world. What Stacy needed most was to focus on *Practical Joy* to bring peace and healing into her life. I helped her reconnect with her love of gardening, and it became her savior.

She took to her yard and began noticing the rhythms of her day, of life, and the animals in the garden. She built relationships with a Western Scrub Jay family. The mama bird even began flying through her open bedroom window each morning to sing to her from the end of the bed.

Planting seeds and nurturing them to grow became a powerful metaphor for the healing that was taking place within her body and soul. The simple act of returning to her joy of gardening changed Stacy's life and helped her heal through presence, reflection, and everyday intention. What passion project could you start or rediscover?

# Joy Journey
## *Three*

### Exploring Passion Projects

Grab a cup of tea or a glass of wine. It's time to dream again.

Take a look at the list of potential passion projects I've started below. Which items intrigue you? Which ones spark a little curious joy? Which ones make you pause and reflect on a memory from your past? Which ones would you be willing to explore further just because?

Circle all that FEEL interesting. Remember to let your heart (not your brain) be your guide! Then, continue brainstorming possible passion project ideas you *might* like to try.

- Bread baking
- Quilting
- Bird watching
- Watercolor painting
- Herb gardening
- Poetry writing

- _____
- _____
- _____
- _____
- _____
- _____
- _____
- _____
- _____
- _____
- _____

- _____
- _____
- _____
- _____
- _____
- _____
- _____
- _____
- _____
- _____

It's important for me to share with you that I believe our cell phones have robbed most of us of our passion projects (and joy). I don't know about you, but it's so easy for me to collect ideas on Pinterest of art I want to create, yet never find the time to actually create. The same with interesting recipes and fun ideas for decorating my home. As much as I love my cell phone, I must be conscious of the amount of time I'm using it. I'd much rather be painting rocks and spreading joy, than pinning ideas and scrolling aimlessly.

*Woohooohooo!*
*Now that you've identified some new (or renewed)*
*passion project ideas, it's time to actively commit*
*to more curiosity and play each day.*

# Notes

*Notes*

Notes

# Your Personal Joy List

## Chapter Four

We all experience pivotal moments that have the potential to turn our lives around—if we listen to the feelings and take aligned action. I call these turning point moments. This particular story is one that still makes me weep tears of gratitude, because this moment was one that changed my life and put me on my personal journey of joy.

Six years ago I was sitting at our kitchen table in Brooklyn, and I was in a total funk. You know this feeling, right? Slightly depressed, gray, agitated, teary, tired, and uninspired by current circumstances. Yet nothing was "wrong." My marriage was great, my business was doing well, and my health was fine.

I pulled out my journal to attempt to work through my feelings, and before I knew it, my tears were mixing with the ink, and I couldn't stop sobbing.

My body was shaking, my breath stuck in my chest. My spouse knelt down next to me and gently asked me what was going on.

The words that came out shocked both of us: "I don't know how to have fun anymore."

It was true. I didn't. I was consumed by work, goals, and to-do lists. I was constantly looking ahead to the next achievement. I had lost the joy of living.

If this resonates with you, you are not alone. We need to help people unravel the "achieve more, do more, be more" that we have learned to equate to happiness in this society. We must unwind our worth from our work. This is a bold act of courage. It takes time to reprogram ourselves from years of societal conditioning, but this is some of the most important work we can do if we want to live a joy-filled life.

What's on the other side, once the unraveling and transformation happens?

Joy. Presence. Laughter. Connection to your soul purpose (which most likely has nothing to do with your work/career). Slowing down. Deep peace. Grace. Ease. Flow.

These are just a few of the qualities lying dormant within you right now. They want to be alive, activated, and awakened—but you must do the unraveling first.

At one of my lowest points at that kitchen table, I did the only thing that made sense to me at the time. I wrote the numbers 1 through 50 on a piece of paper and went on a quest to come up with fifty things that brought me joy.

Sounds simple, right?

This was so difficult for me, and it is also quite difficult for most of the people I work with. Somewhere along the way through parenthood, pleasing others, working hard in our careers/businesses, and everything in between, we've become disconnected from our joy.

But I've got great news for you: you can start the process of reconnecting to joy by creating your own personal joy list, just like I did!

# Joy Journey
## *Four*

## Creating Your Joy List

Creating that joy list was the initial tool that changed everything for me, and since then I have shared this exercise with people around the globe to help them shift back to joy-filled living.

You may experience tears as you reconnect to the simple things that you've forgotten. And you might experience sadness or disappointment if you struggle making "a simple list." This isn't so simple, but loads of joy will greet you on the other side, I promise.

You may need to do this activity in spurts over a few days. Keep your list close. Add to it as you become intentional about bringing joy to the forefront of your life and new things come to you. If you get stuck, take a breath and come back to it. Flip back to your passion project list from Joy Journey #3 and see what you can carry forward to this one.

*What brings you joy? What makes you feel light, carefree, and relaxed? What makes your heart smile?*

As you begin making your list, it is important that FEEL into each entry. The idea here is to capture two aspects: 1) the item and 2) the feeling it evokes and/or the associated memory.

For example, here are a few of mine:

1. Sunrises feel like fresh starts and new possibilities
2. Morning lattes remind me of my mom's kitchen
3. Reading fiction allows me to get lost in another world

1. _____
2. _____
3. _____
4. _____
5. _____
6. _____
7. _____
8. _____
9. _____
10. _____
11. _____
12. _____

*Well done!*
*You now have a go-to list of personalized joy that is meaningful and relevant to you.*

# Notes

# Joy Is a Practice

## Chapter Five

When I teach or speak about the joy-filled life, people are often surprised to learn that joy is a practice. What does that mean exactly?

Ever taken up a new hobby or sport? Perhaps yoga, or flute, or painting, or parenting?! How do you get better at anything? When you become intentional about it *and* you practice it often, that is where the improvement is visible!

I'm not a parent; like Jill whom you met in the beginning of this book, that was an intentional (and wildly unpopular) choice I made in my early thirties. But I do have seven nieces and nephews, and I've learned a lot about children from spending time with them, as well as serving as a public school teacher for fifteen years.

The only way I got better at communicating and understanding these wonderful children was through practice. I messed up a lot! I reflected on my words and actions when they didn't achieve what I had in mind, and the next opportunity I had I tried again—with slight (and sometimes drastic!) adjustments.

Did you know your joy is like this too? It's a practice: a daily intention, a daily choice, a daily decision. There's some trial and error, too. If you want a more joy-filled life, it's important to try things out, explore, and reflect deeply on what truly brings you joy. Once your joy is conscious, you can keep choosing joy day in and day out. Even when it's hard. Even when you don't feel joyful. Even when you're tired, grieving, or uninspired (especially then)!

Your joy matters.

It matters to your emotional, physical, and spiritual well-being. It matters to your family, your friends, and your community. When you choose joy, your energy expands, and everyone around you is positively impacted. A more joyful world starts with me, you, and those we interact with daily.

Ever since connecting to and following her joy, Stephanie has gone back to starting each day with an intentional joy practice. After making her joy list, she realized just how much she loved two things: knitting and coffee. Now, every morning starts with her knitting and coffee practice, and that 20 minutes sets the tone for her day. Stephanie is an artist who enjoys making things with her hands. She enjoys the softness of the fiber, the color, the texture, and the meditative aspect of knitting. She loves being with her thoughts, feeling into her body, and setting the intention for her day. Coffee and knitting is her antidote to spending the rest of the day on a computer!

How might your days flow with more joy and ease if you implemented small joyful practices and became more intentional about living a joy-filled life?

## Joy Journey
### *Five*

### Developing Daily Joy Practices

Let's create some go-to joy practices for you based on your joy list, passion projects, and hierarchy of lifestyle values. Look back at Joy Journeys #2, #3, and #4 and find some things you enjoy or would like to spend more time doing. Identify ones you could group together to create your personalized joy practices.

*Create three joy practices that you can incorporate throughout your day. Be intentional about choosing the time of day that each practice would be a joyful addition to your schedule and also make note of the reason you are pairing up these items. I've given you a few of mine for inspiration.*

Remember, you can tweak and make adjustments as you find pairings that make you feel calm, relaxed, joyful, inspired, and expansive.

My Example:

| TIME OF DAY | JOY PRACTICE | REASON |
|---|---|---|
| Morning | latte and watercolor | I love starting my day with calm, color, and creativity. |
| Afternoon | plated lunch and terrace time | When I was a teacher, I was lucky to even eat lunch. I love sitting in the sunshine, taking a midday pause. |
| Evening | fiction and a cup of tea | Oh, to get lost in a great book. This has become my favorite wind-down routine. |

| TIME OF DAY | JOY PRACTICE | REASON |
|---|---|---|
|  |  |  |
|  |  |  |
|  |  |  |

*You did it! Remember, joy is a choice, a practice, and a lifestyle. All the joy in the world is yours, if and when you decide to prioritize it and live it daily!*

Notes

Notes

# Nature and Joy

## Chapter Six

One of the most practical ways to experience joy is to fall in love with nature. Falling in love with nature requires slowing down and noticing the extraordinary in the ordinary. It's quite a magical practice.

On the days when I feel the most anxiety and heaviness with all that is going on in the world, I spend extra time in nature. I sit on a large shiny rock, letting the earth's warmth radiate through me. I match my breathing to the ebb and flow of the water. I let the sand sift through my fingers, like an hourglass, feeling the graininess of each piece. I literally stop and smell the roses. I track a bird in flight for as long as my eyes can see it. I pick up a blade of grass and examine it as if I've never seen or touched one before.

I truly believe nature has been my biggest teacher of joy. I've learned that every aspect of the natural world has its own divine timing. That going slow, like the waning of the moon, or raging with activity, like a hurricane, are equally beautiful and necessary. These observations have helped me keep balance and perspective on how our lives actually ebb and flow, all in divine timing.

Being present with nature's cycles, grace and fury, simplicity and complexity, continues to show me that a joy-filled life is about perspective, intentionality, and gratitude for what *is*. Being grateful for what currently *is* keeps us present and in a state of choice.

What will you choose today?

# Joy Journey
## *Six*

### Pausing with Nature

How can nature reveal gifts of joy that you may have overlooked in the everyday busyness of life? What might shift within you if you slowed way down and connected to something right outside your door? Let's find out!

Find a small gift from nature, such as a seashell, leaf, acorn, or flower petal. Use as many senses as you can to be present with this object. Sketch or write about what you notice when you examine it closely.

Take a moment to reflect on this practice of slowing down and noticing. How does being deeply present help you connect to your joy?

*Coming back to center happens when you slow down and get grounded in being present. Carry this simple practice with you as you continue your joy journey!*

# Notes

Notes

Notes

# Home as Sanctuary

## Chapter Seven

For too many years, I lived in homes that were not 100 percent me (and therefore not joyful). Our Queens subterranean studio apartment (that's fancy realtor speak for "basement") didn't have enough light. The Brooklyn apartment was too small (a whopping "spacious" 750 square feet). I also tolerated these types of things for far too long: a misshapen sofa, bath towels that were too scratchy, and bare beige walls. Finally, I had had enough.

Maria and I have spent the last two years on a shared project we call Home as Sanctuary. We have painted walls with bright colors, replaced a garden tub with a hot tub, splurged on Egyptian bamboo cotton washcloths and bath towels, and planted seasonal flowers and herb gardens on our terrace. My home office is exactly how I want it: a colorful round rug, meaningful artwork from friends across the globe, and an altar complete with incense, my beloved statue of Ganesha, and a gratitude candle I light each morning.

Putting intentional focus and energy into making your home the most joyful place you can imagine will improve your attitude and quality of life. What would make your home feel more like a sanctuary for you?

Is it a dedicated yoga or painting space, new appliances, a better organization system for your spices, new bedding? Whatever it is, your home should feel like a direct reflection of you, filled with things that bring you joy!

Let's take a little trip around your home and discover how to create an even more joyful sanctuary.

## Joy Journey
## *Seven*

### Sprinkling More Joy Throughout Your Home

Take a walk around your home. Stand in the center of each room and jot down your ideas.

- **What do you love?**
- **What annoys you?**
- **What would you like to add/change?**

The next step is to make changes (large or small) based on your responses. That closet full of clothes and shoes that is driving you nuts? Figure out the next best step so that when you walk into that closet the next time, you smile. That dead plant that makes you sad? Get rid of it—and visit a local nursery to find something that is vibrant and alive!

You are on your way to experiencing more joy than ever before in your home!

Intentionally treating your home as sanctuary helps you remember that joy is absolutely something you can sprinkle more of into your life—whenever and wherever you choose!

## Living Room

## Kitchen

## Bedroom

## Bathroom

# Notes

_____

_____

_____

_____

_____

_____

_____

_____

_____

_____

_____

_____

_____

_____

_____

_____

_____

_____

_____

_____

_____

_____

_____

*Notes*

# Notes

# In the End, Your Joy Is Your Responsibility

My education and science background reinforce my personal code of ethics to use research-based methodologies and collect data and results, so I can tweak tools and ideas before ever rolling out the frameworks for others to use. This is why I stated earlier that all the tools in this book have been tried, true, and tested for years prior to publishing this book.

A few years ago, I experienced a huge change in my marriage. My husband of nearly nine years transitioned to my wife, and early in this transition (of ourselves and our relationship), there were periods characterized by depression, disillusionment, and distress for life as I had once known it. Those un-joyful states lasted off and on for nearly two years, and I am pleased to now share that Maria and I have found our own joy journey in marriage once again. However, this tumultuous time gave me the opportunity to test the *Practical Joy* tools once again. I used each tool in this book to help me rediscover my joy, recommit to it, and practice it daily.

It's been an honor to work with a variety of people helping them (re)discover their joy—and some of them arrived with medical diagnoses such as moderate to severe depression and bipolar disorder. My intent is to always advocate for joy, and I do recognize that these practices are not a replacement for therapy, prescription medications, or other tools that may be medically necessary. Even in these types of circumstances, however, many people did experience more consistent joy when they did the inner work to identify and understand

Conclusion

their hierarchy of lifestyle values and develop daily joy practices to enrich their lives. They often shared this overarching idea with me: My joy matters, despite my diagnosis.

Quanisha is a dear friend who first came to me as a business client. Throughout our work together, she has continued to focus on building a more joyful life while navigating bipolar disorder. When Quanisha creates time to engage in her passion projects, makes business and personal decisions based on her hierarchy of lifestyle values, and incorporates joy practices into her daily life, she remembers that much of her joy is within her control.

As you embark on your own joy journey to (re)discover and commit to a daily joy practice, it's imperative that you remember these key points:

1. **Your joy is a daily practice.** It is your responsibility to discover what brings you joy, to focus on adding more joy to your life, and to cultivate your joy by choosing it again and again and again.
2. **Your joy is contagious.** When you embody joy and live it daily, people will notice the change. They will ask you why you are so happy (because they don't yet realize the difference between joy and happiness). They will ask you for advice on living a more joyful life. Warning: You are about to become contagious in the best of ways!
3. **Your joy is limitless.** You can have more of it anytime you desire. This, of course, requires you to dive into the tools again, uncovering and rediscovering new parts of yourself, connecting to the clearer vision you have for your life, and recommitting to your joy, daily.

My hope is that you experience way more joy than you ever knew was possible. That you create ripples of joy across your community. That you *take it to the people.*

And that together, we raise the consciousness of the planet by choosing joy, each and every day, in the most practical of ways.

# Behind the Scenes Bonus Content

Join Shannon as she takes you behind the scenes with bonus interviews, insight and commentary on the book illustrations and design, and additional interactive content. Simply scan the QR code and dive in!

## Author Q&A

**Q:** What was the moment you knew you needed to seek out more joy?

**A:** Honestly, probably in high school. This was a rough time for me, complete with mean-spirited girls who loved to gossip, sports teams riddled with drama, and small-town mentality. I just didn't fit in anywhere! I remember making a checklist on notebook paper that I would use to assess each day: Did I give someone a compliment today? Did I create time to be alone with my thoughts and feelings? Did I do my best today? This checklist kept me grounded and intentional, and was probably an early version of this book, now that I think about it!

**Q:** What are some of your other favorite books about joy?

**A:** My all-time favorite book, which has helped me deepen my own joy practice, is *The Tao of Joy Everyday* by Derik Lin. I've read this daily devotional at least four times–especially in times of grief and turbulence. Danielle LaPorte's book, *The Desire Map: A Guide to Creating Goals with Soul*, has helped me immensely to identify the way I want to feel each day. She calls these traits "core desired feelings." And I can't leave out *The Book of Joy: Lasting Happiness in a Changing World* by Dalai Lama and Desmond Tutu. This book is a beautiful illustration of how to heal the world using joy and compassion as primary tools for finding joy in every day.

**Q:** What role does community play in cultivating personal joy?

**A:** This is such an important question. I believe we have done much harm to ourselves in thinking: "I got this" and "I am self-sufficient." I've actually been considering this a lot lately–the societal conditioning here in the U.S. of self-sufficiency, and how much it has actually separated us from developing deep relationships and being immersed in true communities that lift us up. I also believe social media plays a huge role in this phenomena as well, allowing us to believe we have "friends" and "connections". While online communities are important to many of us, my current joy practice has included finding communities in my own neighborhood. There is nothing like being with other people who can walk, cook, create art, or cry with you when necessary!

**Q:** What inspired you to illustrate this book?

**A:** Coming back to my art has been a long, painful journey, but I was committed to healing the pieces of me that dismissed my own artistry. Over the last several years, I worked with countless coaches, therapists, and teachers to reignite my creative fire in terms of my art. It wasn't always easy, because I had to rewrite lots of negative stories I was telling myself; however, when I busted through my trauma and blocks - whoa baby! - my creative practice has never been more prolific! When it came time to write *Practical Joy*, I knew I wanted this book to be a joyful and interactive experience for my readers–and to me that meant including whimsical, hand-drawn images! I had to have some stern talks with the gremlins in my head who told me I couldn't illustrate my own book - but alas, here we are! I hope you have fun interacting and coloring the pages.

**Q:** How do you find joy in times of adversity?
**A:** This is such a beautiful question. My daily joy practice is just that - *a practice*. That means I practice it even when times are heavy with grief, anxiety, or sadness, by using rituals and rewards. We have meaningful tools and structures available that we can use over and over again, to experience moments of increased comfort, peace, and hope, even when we may not be experiencing joy in the present moment. My hope is that readers take time to develop their own meaningful joy practice, so they too can experience relief from the heaviness of life, when necessary.

## Group Reading Guide

1. Which of the joy journeys resonated most with you?
2. Which joy journeys brought up feelings of resistance–and why?
3. If you could transport yourself into one of the illustrations, and live in that drawing, which one would you choose and why?
4. Are you experiencing any resistance to adding color to the coloring pages?
5. Shannon says "Your joy is your responsibility." Do you agree or disagree with that statement?
6. If you've been traveling your own joy journey, how did *Practical Joy* make you feel?
7. Who is the most joyfully contagious person in your life right now?
8. What thoughts do you have about the difference between happiness and joy?
9. Were you surprised about how you arranged your hierarchy of lifestyle values?
10. How does your joy make the world a better place?

# *Joyful Business Revolution*™

## Our Commitments

### To our clients...

**Growing Your Business...for GOOD!**
We are committed to helping coaches and consultants grow a joyful and profitable business they love–where abundant time off is non-negotiable.

### To our industry...

**Changing the Industry...for GOOD!**
We are committed to eliminating fear-based messaging, manipulative marketing, and high-pressure selling in the coaching industry...replacing these harmful tactics with #KindMessaging, Education-Based Marketing, and Soulful Selling.

### To our humanity...

**Elevating the Consciousness...for GOOD!**
We believe in diversity, inclusion, justice, and equity for ALL. We support the dismantling of white supremacy and patriarchy, and we are an LGBTQAI2S+ inclusive community.

We are committed to creating supportive and diverse solutions within the company to nurture a culture that is inclusive for our team and clients. We are also committed to creating equal rights and social justice for ALL.

*Here are the services we provide to help coaches and consultants grow their businesses for GOOD:*

- **Messaging Mentorship**: We'll revolutionize your messaging, so that you create unforgettable content that lands you clients.
- **Marketing Mentorship**: We'll revolutionize your marketing, so you intentionally design curated experiences that call in your dream clients.
- **Scaling Mentorship**: We'll revolutionize your leadership, so you grow a world-class brand that leaves a legacy.
- **Messaging & Marketing Intensive**: We'll revolutionize one program/ offer you have already developed, so you can reintroduce it to your community and sell more of it!

*We invite you to connect with us at www.joyfulbusinessrevolution.com.*

# Spread the JOY!

If you've been inspired and moved by *Practical Joy*, here are some easy ways to help spread the joy, any of which I will be grateful for:

1. Send me an email or video testimonial: info@practicaljoybook.com
2. Post quotes or reviews on Facebook, Instagram, or your favorite social media channel. Or go old school: Fly a banner from a plane! Rent a billboard!
3. Review the book on any online bookseller's site.
4. Review the book on your website.
5. Start a *Practical Joy* Book Club. Use the Group Reading Guide section to enrich your discussions.
6. Buy a few copies of the book and send joyful snail mail to your friends and family!
7. Invite me to speak to your organization, at your event, or to your community about joy. Please send your inquiry to info@practicaljoybook.com
8. Order bulk copies (more than 10) by sending an email request to info@practicaljoybook.com. We support organizations that spread joy!

# Acknowledgments

When I knew it was time to write this book, it had to be done in an environment that was 100% joyful. For me, this meant sitting on a beach in Mexico, writing on a yellow notepad with my favorite blue ink pen, and eating chips and guacamole as my daily reward for writing!

I am grateful for my dear friend Amy Civica, who cooked for me while I was in Mexico, so I could pour all my energy and focus into the book, and still be nourished in body and soul with her delicious food. I am forever grateful for Toni Lynn Pakus who took the photocopied notepad pages and typed them out for me, because more time at a computer was definitely not feeling joyful. Thank you to both Dr. Minette Riordan and Stacy Louise Christopher who have helped me heal so many years of wounds and blocks around creativity, and who nurtured me with their loving guidance, so I could illustrate this book with beautiful coloring pages that will bring joy to many!

There was only one choice for me when it came time to partner with a publishing professional, and that choice was Susie Schaefer! She has been an advocate of my joy work for many years, and the "cause publishing" model she teaches aligns with my highest values of generosity and giving back. Big thanks to Amy Scott, my editor, who also has championed this body of work for years! Amy's expertise in editing helped make this book the best version of itself.

Finally, thank you to Maria, my lovely spouse, and all my students and clients, who continue to come back to these teachings, find their joy, and remind me to do the same when needed.

Acknowledgments

# Joy Scholarship Fund

As all of these stories and joy journeys demonstrate, we have the potential to increase our joy in the most practical of ways–and make the world a better place because of our daily joy practice. A portion of the proceeds of book sales from *Practical Joy* will be allocated to the Joy Scholarship Fund at the Joyful Business Revolution™. This allows us to continue teaching and inspiring others to cultivate their joy in life and business, so they can create joy ripples around the world that impact and reach many.

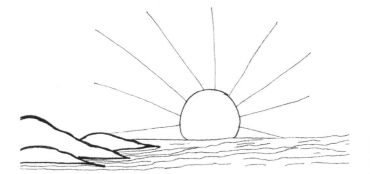

# About the Author

M. Shannon Hernandez is ALL ABOUT THAT JOY in life and biz. She is specifically known around the globe for The Content Personality® Wheel and E.X.P.A.N.D. Method™. Shannon is the founder of Joyful Business Revolution™ where she and her team partner with online coaches and  consultants to teach them how to grow their business for GOOD, resulting in more joy, more time-off, and more profit with purpose.

A sought-after expert in the world of online business strategy, Shannon has been featured on CBS, ABC, FOX, and NBC. She has founded The Content Personality® Club, The Confident Expert™ Program, and The Joyful CEO™ Mastermind Program, where she and her team rally coaches and consultants to grow their profits—while increasing their impact.

Shannon has over 25 years in award-winning curriculum design, working with both the NFL & U.S. Military, as a master trainer and teacher. She is committed to ongoing philanthropic work to bring housing, fresh food and water sources, and medical care to those without access. When not speaking and teaching globally, Shannon is reading fiction, snuggling her cat, traveling the world, spreading joy, and hanging with the love of her life, Maria.

Made in the USA
Las Vegas, NV
10 December 2024

13828760R00066